Blind Uncle Night

Blind Uncle Night

Poems by Art Homer

CW Books

Published by CW Books
P.O. Box 541106
Cincinnati, OH 45254-1106

ISBN: 9781936370788
LCCN: 2012940488

Poetry Editor: Kevin Walzer
Business Editor: Lori Jareo

Visit us on the web at www.readcwbooks.com

Cover photo credit: Alison Wilson
Digital enhancement: James Sewing

Acknowledgements

Grateful acknowledgment is made to the following publications in which these poems originally appeared, some in slightly different form.

Antioch Review for "Charlie Christian and the Birth of the Hip"; *Blackbird* for "Buck with a Broken Horn," and "Least Terns at Beaver Lake"; *Poetry* for "Nocturne Moderne," and "Pikuni Free School; *Green Mountain Review* for "Three Day California Honky Tonk Weekend"; *Southern Poetry Review* for "Pawnshops"; *The Journal* for "Bucky Takes Time Off"; *The Lyric* for "Poor Old Art," *Prairie Schooner* for "i'm not he is"; *1993 Poets Market* and *The Art and Craft of Poetry* by Michael Bugeja. (F&W Publications, 1994) for "At the Heartland Cafe"; *Second Helpings: More Eating Nebraska* (Pleasant Dale Press, 1996) for "Lunch at Jams Grill, Omaha, Nebraska"; *Chariton Review* for "Festival," "Turkey Vultures," and "John Clare, Bring Your Fiddle"; *Great River Review* for "All Saints, South Omaha, "Valentines Day"; *Madison Review* for "Escape"; *Poetry Southeast* for "Survivors:" *Fifth Wednesday Journal* for "Gastaõ Bueno Lobo" and "Ones and Threes, Twos and Fours."

Special thanks to The University of Nebraska at Omaha for a professional development leave during which some of these poems were written

For John and Betty Wilson,
and, always
for Alison.

Table of Contents

I. The Animals

I think I could turn and live with animals, they are so
                    placid and self-contain'd,
I stand and look at them long and long.

—Walt Whitman, *Song of Myself*

Turkey Vultures

The majority of the Universe—some 70%—is
composed of dark energy, an equally mysterious
quantity which exerts negative pressure.
from *"Team Finds 'Proof' of Dark Matter"*—
BBC News Service

Given wind enough these big birds
go acrobat, six foot plus of wing,
negative space against the year's first
thunderheads southwest.
                                        Barrel roll,
stall turn, everything short of loop.
Migrate by maintaining stall against
prevailing wind, wait a week for sun
and bloat to cook your meat, and you'd
stand on one wing in the face of storms
that emit lightning and a galaxy of cloud
and homeowners, pulling their sheets
off lines, colliding with their own
trash and patio furniture, the pulverized
receipts of dead deals blown from offices
of seed salesmen, cabs of grain trucks.

Vultures must absorb light, draggled stars
parked on snags and fence posts till the dew
evaporates from wing and back, must launch
themselves into thick air while blackbirds
and kingbirds strafe their bald grey pates.
Safe in the updrafts, they maintain their
septic orbit over the bluffs. I watch them
for the good news: uplift.
                                        Let the field sparrows'

13

cries rebound, the bluebirds and the cardinals
rejoice. Gouts of empty space, the vultures wheel
above them, lenses through the false blue
to all that lies beyond. What does the dark
matter if they are not afraid? Clouds gather
themselves unto themselves until we cannot
read their intent or direction. Safe in wind,
they know that clinging to the earth
is the surest way to be pulled apart.

Least Terns at Beaver Creek

Mewling called me out of daydream,
halfway between the gas pump and the steel
wall of convenience mart. Surprised sky
unfurled the flock, a tumbled bag of jacks, cards
shuffled by an errant wind and let go. The black
wedge of wingtip, flipped against the white
beneath, creates a stripe against which words
may be concealed. One such word is history,
but I don't know what to think of it because
the birds are rolling into the curls
and breakers of air
above fresh-planted swells of soil,
the hill against the sky interring calm
as transept to migration of vowels or genes,
these determined words shouldering the climate
and eons into breeding frenzy.

There is no ocean near. The lake is lake in name only,
a reservoir in land drier than it knows. I am trawling
the home stretch for courage
and find it in these envelopes of warmth,
no larger than the pockets I search for keys,
cards, money to pay the clerk who stands waiting,
no doubt wondering why this regular is stalled,
stunned, and smiling to conspirators
parked somewhere overhead.

Buck with a Broken Horn

First your ribs, your half-fleshed face, a hip socket
cocked above blown leaves—I call my eager pup
to "leave it"—then your rack, atypically narrow,
four points by the western count, sans eyebrow tine,
and finally the broken stump of your right horn
reminds me of the coyote chorus here two weeks ago.
Such jubilation that the owls fell silent.

It could have been the fourteen-point buck
that broke this near the base, a misplaced shot
from some early season hunter. I vote
for Mr. Big, killed days ago and processed
into steaks and summer sausage.
If I go hungry, neighbors say, it's my own fault,
because you'll feed us all, coyote, man, the lust
of does for stronger genes, and in the cold that waits
this year till spring to settle on the land,
the thousand gnawing teeth of mice,
and finally the land itself.

Walking the Pup

This slant of light quarters into wind.
Beans sprout in hot November fields
the combines left for chisel plows, for rain
that never fell, for the deer carcass
and five hides to distract pup at windrow.
Under the bib of wooded bluff, river mist
milks morning for the last, damp filter
of horizon, setting redtails in one cottonwood
after another into their hoarse cry and float
over neighboring corn, waste shucked
and lying bait to coon and possum,
deer and pheasant, ears big
as retrieving dummies for the brown
pup to mark and find.
                          We aren't here
for form, simply to walk the bottom
where meat hunters leave deer hides
amongst the shattercane and wetland brush—
here to learn what it means to be
together, to move in concert up
the dike and through marshy ground,
across the mounded dirt of windrows
with the sudden snap of saplings
against chest and leg. Along the civic trail,
a stand of locust whets the air with thorns
long as my fingers, a tangle of treble hooks,
a child's jacks waiting for some tricky retrieve—
waiting like us for the focus that comes
to those who choose earth, here black and shining
where the plow has dug a drain to move
more water to the culvert.
                          And as if the thought
of drainage parched the morning, the air

goes dry as oak ash, mist turned smoke and sealed
into another patch of sketchy cover,
timothy and elm sprouts concealing nothing
but this year's dearth of birds.

Valentines Day

Downhill from the pawpaw patch
the yellowjacket nest lay half in a muddy
deer track, half in the layer of leaves—
white oak, bur oak, but few of the pawpaw
leaves themselves. The year has been so dry
the leaves hold their shape yet, and the mud
is from the first rain and light snow that
has surprised even the deer. I imagine
the misstep that left this gash in the hillside,
the deer panicked by the ground's sudden
liquidity where she had invested her weight
all winter without thought. Maybe she clipped
the ash or young oak that held the nest,
or maybe it fell sodden with the last
leaves now pasted into the collage
of its outer shell.

And maybe this is why I pick it up,
carry it through woods, over the hill,
across two fields and back, circling
the Romeo and Juliet pond.
This dry year, deer leave little track
in hard clay—all that's left
of the shallows where we warned Hooch
off the pond's namesakes, two
snapping turtles, who at first looked dead,
then cataleptic in their slow mating.

Maybe because this is the driest
year in sixty, the planted
pines in neighbors' drives
succumbing to wilt, crops good
only for silage, and cattle eating the wild

roses we've named our farm for—
maybe this is reason enough to carry
this torn volume of tissue back
and into the house we've built—
as much as time, talent, and law allows—
ourselves, and hold it up for you to ask:
"Why are you giving me this?"

Frog Being Eaten by a Snake

cries like a kitten. "Catbird,"
I tell myself, though I know better,
and spend the time between throwing
a stick into the pond
and Daisy's loud retrieve
searching the tops of ash and basswood,
drowned snag and live willow.

Tender hearted and soft mouthed,
she is a dog easy to love as pie,
as welcoming as the smell of wood smoke
and apple after a long day away,.
When we first heard this sound,
she sniffed an old pile of lumber
until I overturned a board.
A garter snake had one

leg of a tree frog swallowed—
the other forced past its head
for easier passage. Daisy whined,
and I found a switch of cottonwood
to flail the snake. When they both
struggled off in different directions,
Daisy walked off, looking back at me.
I know, I said. They'll probably both
be eaten by birds, but at least
the screaming has stopped.

Logging Chain with Broken Links
Occasional Haiku and Renga

i First Scent of Snow

Snow on the mountain
reminds me of Montana.
Snow on the mountain.

Deer bed in field of spring grass—
dark dimple in wind's sine waves.

ii '70 International Harvester

Bluebird six engine,
two ton rear end with dump box;
I'm a happy man.

iii 21st Century

Faith, politics, sports.
Overpopulation looms.
We keep playing games.

Probe lands on Titan:
on morning news shows—nothing.

iv Seven Stitches

Knife slips. Below the heel
of my palm, a pad of fat—
white as packing foam.

v Hunting Morels

Scraped off on piss elm,
tufts of rain-glazed deer hair show

travel direction.

vi Mud Dauber

Industrious wasp,
you're building your home in mine.
Reason to kill? Yes.

vii Fiery Skipper Butterfly

Wing-flicker through green
blades of spring warns me: *don't set*
grass on fire again.

viii Lost Items

Basho translation,
logging chain with broken links—
I'll need them someday.

Snow on the Mountain:
or Life Amongst the Tree-Haters

Snow on the Mountain: annual spurge of western United States having showy white-bracted flower clusters and very poisonous milk. A stand of this on a hillside gives the appearance of the ground being covered with snow - thus the name.
                    —USDA guide to noxious weeds.

Ghost weed of waste areas, it sells in catalogs
next to its cousin, poinsettia. We ignore
the weed guide, pick it without care for the milk
said to burn like poison ivy. Snow
on the mountain, snow on the prairie,
pollinated by flies and short-tongued bees...
one friend asked her husband
why we had so many more wild flowers.
We practice weed control.

Unlike us, unlike Rich, near tears,
watching farmers kill the only
native evergreens, Eastern red cedar,
the blush of berries a tonic
autumn mornings. But junipers
compete with cows for forage,
blaze up in grass fires to ignite
oak and walnut—"High dollar trees"
that can be logged each generation.

Baled in hay, the flowers we cut
can kill a cow. Sear the ends to keep
"snow in summer," another name,
another guidebook. Volunteers work
a hundred miles of river bluffs all fall,

cutting invasive trees, stacking them
in fragrant piles. In the fire kill, in shaded
ground where cedars stood, in grazed-
out lots, and the calcareous soil
of salt-wracked roadsides...snow
on the mountain, snow on the mountain,
snow on the mountain.

Coyote

The coltish pup crosses Honey Creek Road
from one green wall of corn to the other, sits
in an alcove of flattened stalks, shakes ears
it hasn't grown into. Here three days on its own,
it leaves me guessing— orphan? male seeking
his fate? This healthy pup shows mange
has run its course for now, and end to finding
skeletons crows and buzzards drag
through ironweed, the skull at last abandoned
even by the gnawing mice. One big male
stood at the top of a road cut early last winter,
coat a heavy cape about his shoulders and head,
hindquarters scabbed leather. I rarely see
Mangy coyotes hit by cars. I think
they crawl away to die. Water in ponds
turns over each spring, and seasons cycle:
rabbits and foxes, then a coyote year.

I think of their mincing ways, how they gorge
on wild plums and shit piles of pits—
the screams of the young raccoon caught in grass
by the hungry pack. The next day my dog
found skeleton and skin,
                              how I once mistook
their chorus for a squad of cheerleaders.
Far out in the country, afoot, our truck
broken down, underdressed, my wife and I
walked toward them for a moment. I thought
of a football field at dusk, over the hill,
the lights not yet turned on—of two country
schools, rivals for years. Surely, there would be
pickups back of the bleachers, jumper cables
snarled in the back. "Coyotes" I said a few

steps later, and we walked closer together,
toward the house of survivalists
who helped us on our way.

Two or three times a year I hear their cries
from bed. Soon, Daisy the Lab will find
the carcass of a rut-injured buck the pack
has finished off, or a single leg of fawn
less than a football field away from the lawn
I mow as firebreak. "Leave it," I cry,
and she does. I have friends who want to know
the point of my stories about coyotes.

Bull Snakes

Unwrapped from sleep on crushed rock,
four feet of dappled rope infers itself
back into the roadside purpletop.
I find another in the last fold of carpet
unrolled on the lawn for the band—
yet another digesting mice behind cased
fonts of type in the unfinished studio.
This is the letter for fear, for the farmer
disabused of reason and swinging as many feet
as he can manage of logging chain,
perfectly aware this is not the rattler
it mimics, waving its anorexic tail in the air
and gargling a long hiss from its narrow lung—
man and snake too stubborn to back down
from the old feud. Rattlers, pit vipers,
have heads like the glans of a bull,
a man-fist daring you to pound this block
and tackle back into its hole.
The bull-snake
is a pin-head, side-show geek that can't bite
the head off a field mouse, has to dislocate
its own jaw to dine, can be killed
by complications from a rodent bite,
by the tiny ring-neck snake, eater
of earthworms.
                    Metaphor for thought
to ancient Egyptians, and for lawyers
in jokes about roadkill—this one,
sunning itself on Honey Creek Road,
has learned from a million years
of evolution one thing, crawls away
at the sound of a pickup in reverse.

Late November

Twenty paces from the kitchen door
night surrounds a beam of porch light.
The first north wind this winter
drives a stream of dry snow
over a cord of oak, red elm and walnut.
Ice and powder glaze the wood.
The earth and still-green grass
give softly underfoot. A wave
of honking ripples through
an early flight of geese.
Look up. A half dozen stars
wink like silver lures
in deep, fast water.

Chainsaws

scare me more than guns, but less
than the power takeoff on a tractor.
Bob just gave my big saw back,
said "you could do some
damage with that." I told him
it tears me up just carrying it around.

When I work around the tractor
I remember the story of the man
who got his overalls caught in the PTO.
At the end of the day, his neighbors
found the tractor running, a hole
beaten into the ground behind it
and a bloody rag flipping
around and around.

Peregrine at Cheddar Gorge
—Somerset, 2002

Our pasture tent site fronts a football club
wild for championship—shearing time,
sheepdog snarling as I climb the stone-
walled fold, pay the owner amidst the wide,
white backs of sheep. In town, teashops sell
lunch alfresco on stone courtyards. A trout
stream springs from caves, a flood of tourists
from coaches taller than houses. The trail lofts us
over old hotels, a restaurant serving game.

Higher, half-wild Soay sheep run loose,
a raven croaks behind a rock. Ruined
sheepfolds, short-cropped grass, pigeons fat
as housecats, rock wall cottages—all signs
of long habitation. From the top, no stream
in sight but tourists stopping at caves whose local
mold made mild cheese famous. Light breeze
cups its hand across the crest. The shriek

of air two feet past my ear leaves barely
time to think "a falcon's stoop." Screams
of pink woodpigeons echo off the rocks.
Suspended between dives,
the peregrine,
in focus for the moment, drops again,
too far off for us to hear the open-
throttled roar. She disappears with speed.
Again the wail of pigeons, till one cry
singles itself out, reminding flocks
and herds below they once were free.

Ones and Threes, Twos and Fours

— an American Primitive requiem for John Fahey

"Learn to catch the catfish, boy" the fat
man said. So I did. I tried. I meant to learn
to sing with any wind. Hit the twos
and fours, but say the ones and threes. I love
to see the evening sun go down, now
that I'm here, now that fields squeeze
another autumn out of purple top
and little bluestem I buzz past on the gas
mower that breaks my back. I'm singing—
thinking of *Cool Hand Luke* "shaking
the bushes boss." Around here they skin
the catfish live and score bony carp
in flakes that fool the pallet. You're eating
the bones and don't know it" Dutch says.

I don't say anything, flip back across
the field and focus on home. Damn that hurts—
joints, knees—it's timing beats the crap
out of me, swing the tune or the axe,
a chord of wood to stack and a bad back.
No time, no time to hit the gong, to wait
for fruit to vine ripen, for lightning to strike
the clothesline, all the work and school clothes
exhaled toward Des Moines in the first cool front,
coda for two-step and shuffle a lecture
on music from two ends of an old world.

This is America, fer crissakes, Nemaha
downstream of Omaha, "upstream" in native
tongue. You've got that swing in your step,
that back beat down, all you know and all you
need, unluckily. A bit of musicology

to hit the breaks and play the bridge, washed
out south of town. It's flash flood warnings
here to Humbolt. Cloud to ground now,
striking the big gong of bedrock to send
dogs under porches, tables, my desk till we call
and hear her thick tale bang the oak legs.
Hold that note. Use your cheeks to force air
past the lips while—always through the nose—
you breathe.

"Dull as Five Miles of Dirt Road,"

I'd say before we lived at the end
of three miles one way, two another.
Deer jink before the car each morning,
on their way to bed, the occasional
coyote testing them for lameness.
Most does trail two fawns so fat
the dimple of their backbones could hold
a quart of rainwater.
                              Three turkey hens
chuck and squall at fifty half-grown
chicks shuttling through the road cut
ahead of one slow white pickup—
"Forty eight," says the woman
talked about in town. "I had a roundup
started here until you broke up my herd."

Two falls back, I herded two bobcat kits
down this same cut, rousted from their play
in the dust of a dry puddle. Their rabbity
gait raised puffs of dust until they broke
left up the embankment.
                              Jealous boyfriends,
thieves, and mountain lions reported
on this road never show themselves to me,
though I have seen a single large cat track
before a neighbor's gate the night their dog barked
but wouldn't go outside. I'm nearly always late
to doctor's appointments, or to coffee klatch in town.
One morning I shouted to the retired farmers,
the college professor, the town maintenance man,
and the waitress: *That's no Cessna; somebody's flown
an airliner into the world trade towers.*
                              "Is that New York,"

Stanley asked "or Boston? I know it ain't
Chicago; I been there." We stayed and watched
till our dull lives called us back, daily chores,
jobs, bills on the kitchen table.
                              Back from the post office,
I passed the stand of beaver-felled cottonwoods
and noticed two more down. The radio announced
collapse, the grounding of all air traffic except
Air Force one, en route from Florida to a secret
location where the President would address the nation.

Above my head, the braided contrail of an airliner
with fighter escort pointed north toward Omaha.
Two weeks before, I'd picked up Whitey,
walking home from his broken tractor.
His head grazed the roof of my small car.
"He's bigger than I thought." I told Dutch
and he said "He'd be a big man
if his legs was longer."
                              Now, the national news
mute, the county bulldozes beaver nests.
A dead starling has been hooked on telephone wire
above the pond for weeks. Each wind shift
moves it east or west, feathers falling off,
eyes dull as five miles of dirt road.

II. Dark of the Moon

and what are you going to do—
what can you do
about it—
deep, blue night?

—Mary Oliver, "Poppies"

Dark of the Moon

i. The Stars

Remember the night without planes, the move
to the country to dance with the night sky.
That old puppet, Orion, marches up
out of Agincourt. Remember the touch
of wood on your shoulder, yew, Osage
Orange, country churchyards,
declination of wall and Ursa Major
aligned with Polaris.

It is hard to sleep, hard to forget
the tasks of the city. What are the old
stories of forgetting? In winter
trees are nothing but root and memory—
here, oak and walnut, the hard
and the dark. The oaks are white
at their centers. The wood burns dry.
Try to be like the oaks. Try
to sleep under the cold stars.

Without forgetting, there is no sleep.
Older than Oaks, deeds, safe
now in the bank vault in town,
say one man sold this land
to have first his wife , then himself
declared incompetent, committed
to a home in the state capitol,
Lincoln, after the president whose
secretary of state signed the land grant,
now in the vault in the town two miles
west, one mile north of this land, this north half
of the northwest quarter of the section, range
and township you have forgotten.

You cannot forget the state.

These somber trees disregard Whitman's
famous wish to live with the animals.
Now that you live with the animals
you wish to be like the trees, never to shiver,
but to sleep through the dark of the moon,
to reach toward the stars, faint
against light leaked from the city,
faint, even in the dark of the moon
with Saturn and Jupiter rising after sunset
for appointments set in motion
(more—no stanza break)
before the stars leaked like light from the city,
waking you to write on the pad on the table:
Keep appointment tomorrow in city.

Turn the pad toward Polaris, turn
it face down on the table. Sleep and forget
the light. Let it leak from the city.

ii. *Coda: The Dark*

The night of national emergency,
grounded planes left stars alone in the sky.
The secretary of state spoke. The president
spoke of the dark soul of man. The land
remained silent in the dark of the moon.
Even coyotes were silent. Fox in den, kenneled
hunting dog sleep, silent as trees, those goblets
for starlight. The dark of the moon
shows itself larger than light, strangles
the weasels of sleeplessness. No wonder
there's no sleep when we see so far
beyond our beginnings into time when we are

no more. There will be time for sleep.
Perhaps we were never awake until now,
when sleep cannot leak from the eyes of light-
blind citizens, asleep in the city or town,
asleep in the dangerous dark
of the moon.

Attic Window

Names that reflect home life are Broken Dishes, Cake
Stand, Basket, Attic Windows...
    —from an online history of quilting

Late in the year a three-quarters moon
rides pale sky like an attic window,
one corner masked by eaves. Someone
has left the light on up there, though

the room has been empty for years.
Maybe a woman has her quilting frame
set up under the rafters. Maybe she hears
her mother saying each quilt's name:

Flock of Geese and Split Rail Fence,
Attic Window, Bears Paw, and Blazing Star.
Why, if every passing month invents
new patterns, does the same moon appear

in every pane? Who's there, distorted face
gaping through the glass? What is this place?

Poor Old Art

Winter sun sends up a rose rinse behind the hill.
If I doubt the century or my age, I remember
I'm driving home in my pickup,
not an oxcart, or shank's mare.

Still, the light is medieval, my mood
spent from the dogged labor
of building a house, haunted
by the words of the insurance man in the town
whose street glow fights sunset for horizon:

"Let's say something happens to poor old Art."

He's speaking to my wife as if, already,
I'm not there. "He's not there," he says.
"Heaven," he says, "forbid" waving hands in air.
We have bought land. We want insurance.
The root of mortgage is death. See where this leads?

I'd like to think she'd remember me fondly, poor old
Art who thought it romantic to drive
an old pickup, to build their own house.
Everyone could see he wasn't much
of a carpenter, though stubborn enough to keep at it
till he'd made a half-way decent job, a monument—
Sort of like the grave of the man neighbors call
"Harry the Jew," standing alone on a knoll outside town
with its white fence and single grave.

                              And though she'd
carry on, take a lover—someone less trouble—
would travel, have the grandkids out, build
a better house, she would smile at the mention of my name,

and give a pleasant thought to the chance I still existed
somewhere. "Art would have loved this,"
she'd say, or "he'd hate that." and laugh at my ill humor.

But just as I'm coming to terms with my demise,
she brings me back. "Art says it's... what is it you
say?" she says, recalling my AWOL spirit from some beyond
it's been traipsing "betting against yourself, because you
have to die to win." And the agent has lost his sale,
though he's right, it is the only safe bet. And poor old Art
has to go back to his imperfect labors, building a house
that may be plumb, but won't be close to square.

The Attic

Here we cast and retrieve shadow
from the current of truss and stud.
I am on a Saturday run for the channel
rain water takes toward blood's trywork.
One vein along the dorsal axis darts
eaves and doorways. Be this prefab
or cruck house, all the finesse of herring-
bone set above the daub and wattle of domestic
maw here diagrams codes our family
shims and dovetails, wheels beneath.

What are our waves? What tack or pitch
takes us across casement and crenellation
to the flinch of colonnade baiting puncheon,
bearing less weight every trip? Insulated
from sky by dead leaves, squirrels sleep,
dapping pools of winter for owls.

By the blood suffocating in my arm,
cocked back on the roof beam, I
tell the land of floating spiders how long
tabled dust must sit before the set
of line, before the spot of rise and take
can mend the tension, pitch or cast where all
intention comes to base and structure. Beak
and claw, timber and nogging, family
and the light sleep of traipsed stringers—
these small leaks I can patch.

Meteor

The tick crawling past my elbow
wakes me from a dream of closed rooms.
I find it, but drop in into sheets,
or back into the tee shirt I wore to bed.
The spring night is cool, the skylight
open to the still air, half moon.
The hair behind my ear rankles. It's
the tick, back to lodge in the hairline.
Again I lose it in the dark. I can't sleep,
but do not want to waken my wife with light.
Besides, touch is truer than sight. My dog
searches her fur with her teeth, I the back
of knee, between the shoulder blades—
hers and mine. But now the house sleeps
and I wait, listen to a duet of barred
owls in a distant hollow, the female's
sigh and flutter, monkey hoot and bark
of male. Finally, I rise and totter
through the darkened house to the false
security of sight, mirrors, bathroom light.

After searching body and clothes, my night
vision shot, I grope for ice water.
Hands full of pitcher and glass, elbow
propping the fridge door open for light,
I feel it at last, the clasp of eight legs
scaling my neck. By late summer, tired
of the pinching and popping, we consign them
to a jar of acetone. Tonight,
I blacken my thumbnail with tick's blood,
return to sleep until the moon has set.

False dawn and whining wake me

for the morning ritual of letting out,
and stargazing while the big lab searches
tall grass for the perfect spot, and the owls
reprise their loony harmony uninterrupted,
even when a southbound meteor
rips a sky that suddenly seems too perfect.
The biggest I have ever seen, it trails
volcanic flame, with a memory of green
and a final flash that has the pup looking
over her shoulder as she races toward me.

Fires Seen from the Highway

Tannic flames and creosote
across Missouri bottomland—
below the overpass two boxcars
throw open their doors
to the Pacific Junction siding.
Loud visitors debark
in fuchsia shirts, dance
in mid-morning sun, bad news
for hung-over motorists.

That night the road jumps
through the hoops of a semi's
brakes aflame on the shoulder.
The driver kneels beside
his rig, the split rims soaking up
heat from his brakes,
till one tire explodes his arm.
A man's death two weeks later
blooms in grain dust firing the elevator.
A lava flow of corn, helicopters
harvest clips for evening news.

Tendons resewn across the bones,
the driver tries to crook *come here*
with his index finger
and the ring finger moves—
like the game of crossed hands,
or the dive a cyclist takes,
swapping left and right on handlebars.
What happens is the body's fire
burns underground like buried roots

and flames into motion
on the opposite hand.

Etude: Latitude by Longitude
(95° 59' 45"W x 41° 14' 45" N—alt. 1106')

Night hawks rank themselves shoulder to shoulder
in the next-to-last south breeze before they clear out.
Already the robins have bathed together in the cutbanks
under the bluffs. The leaves are the color of their breasts
and the commonplaces of fall are showing themselves
more transient than harvest workers or cherry blossoms.
Like hands bearing candles, the leaves drift and build
their own *ofrendas* , their papier-mâché saints and *muertos*.

Once again the savory lawn of my neighbor censors
the air with onion and chives he has mown and stacked
behind my fence. The flavored wind will start again
next spring when the snow drifts thaw. All over town
the Smolskys are telling their children it is time
to grind sausage, trading in pork prices and garlic futures.
New year will cook a thick wort, though I'll have to phone
Tim to confer on hop rates. We've pitched our yeast
but there's a long wait before my lager crowns.

Carboys wait for me to rack ale, shelves to uphold
consequence: few photos, many books. A pot,
well but inexpertly thrown holds orbicular jasper
from the last wilderness beach, Olympic goat hair
with twigs it hung from tangled in the snarls. Clouds
not yet arrived are carded clean above tundra.

Weather matures toward winter under a horizon
bright as semi-precious stone set in metal, enameled
with a few fresh drops of blood. Hunters dress out
their kill. Once or twice a life they must expect

a nick or gash from the skinning knife, to marry their blood with their game's. These are the few days when we have all the time in the world.

Kuiper Belt

At 200 degrees below zero,
water is metal we send
more metal to probe.
A man might see a woman's
body, a woman another's
face in the gray landscapes
of orbiting ice. Sensors
see below the surface, see ice
and conglomerates of dust.
I see the Moai of Easter Island,
faces that are bodies of thought
with appetites that ate all the palms.

We are arriving at these new islands
with our outriggers full of sensors,
our bodies vessels crammed
with seeds and pigs, with taro root
and viruses. No birds circle
our new shores. The distant sunset
ignites no waves. Driven beyond
gardens, home, and sky
we drink our molten metal—
our blood still volatile and hungry.

Five A.M., That Small Problem Again

The moon's a gutted trout awash in dark
current I can't reach. I should sleep.
How blind uncle night baits hooks is none
of my concern. Some fool stuck carp scales
in my eyelid. Now they flash like stars.
Where are coyotes that used to wail steep
arpeggios over the lake? Their words and song
were one quick boat. Look, you can see the sails.

But why should I let sleep wear out my eyes —
one ear to the ground, the other pressed
to air that won't stop galloping in my chest?
The heart canters back and forth from fence
of ribs to open range that always lies
the other side of darkness, dream and silence.

Waking Out of a Fever

Sleep goes tunneling through our lives
with its funny little nose for trouble twitching.
It surfaces day by day where it wishes,
stitching the landscape of our wilderness
lives together like the small burrows
basting urban lawns to woodlots. The owners,
as we all must, dream on. The common
wood rat, the star-nosed mole, these
creatures are our real companions
grubbing along like everyone just a few
football fields away from gang killings
and particle accelerators. Hibernation
mines deep under the English Channel
of winter, and we come up each spring smelling
of dry leaves and salmon smoked in cold
sheds, a petal of the flaky flesh in our teeth
like a meal of rose blossoms.

Escape

—after viewing photos of Hiroshima & Nagasaki

Tonight, the unidentified
sonata wavers over cornfields
from a far station. All day,
shadows of the still-leafed trees
have levered for position.
But this is only one song
shaped by light or lack
like images of victims burnt
into cement at Bantai Bridge.

They're popular images, the shadows
of the Emperor's subjects whose city
became a camera one afternoon.
If we examine their outlines,
eloquent gestures, we catch
a comforting blur that hints of escape.
Their silhouettes whisper off: man
pulling a cart, the shades pale as those
survivors call ghosts gathered at river's
edge to drink deep as burnt deer
after a forest fire. We can think,
hard as it is, of bodies no longer
blocking light, the blurred
edges a sort of steam, not broken
resolution, but too fine a focus —
not souls, but the body rising
out of the body like Eucharist
whispering around a cloud
before they became less than gas.

And the layers of brick, stone —
we are not talking about heat,

about the August one witness called
a series of burning suns, nor wavy lines
off highways. We speak of the day
an emperor became a man,
how flesh and light leapt
straight off the earth as particles,
their existence theoretical, to escape
sun and shadow, to pass through planets
neither slowed nor bent by gravity

III. Country Blues

I'd rather shoot a man than a hawk.

—Robinson Jeffers, "Hurt Hawks"

His blindness . . . the result of a shotgun blast of bird
shot to the face that blew away his eyes during a
drunken argument with a friend near Tallulah,
Louisiana in the mid-1920's . . . did not prevent him
from fending for himself, as he became known as a
crack-shot with a pistol from hearing his target.

—from a biography of Blind Joe Reynolds, bluesman.

Pikuni Free School
Browning Montana

It's the land, what is there to say? I already
wrote about the buffalo, how
they're gone and how it used to be.
I got an A. I seen two or three
at the county fair —from Arlee, some
cousin's ranch for rodeo stock.

Some guy from Missoula come up here.
Read us a poem about somebody finds
a road kill deer. He's worried it's pregnant
so he rolls it off the side. I said why don't
he dress it out if it's that fresh.
                              Then that poetry
guy says you don't understand and gives us
paper, says write about the land. It's full
of graves I say and he says write that down.

Blind Blake

(born Arthur Blake [Phelps???] circa 1893,
Jacksonville FL or Carolina Islands—died circa
1933)

How did you learn to write
"Cordially Yours" on your only photo,
in the same hand that signed Blind Lemon's?

Before drink slowed your sportin'
right hand, fearless before recording horns,
you blazed the Early Morning
Blues, West Coast Blues, "gonna
sing some geechie style" in Southern
Rag, some drop-thumb bass,
root an eighth before the measure.
It was boogie before boogie, a thumb
that swung, like a piano player's whole
left hand.
          And you could stride piano
with Bertha Henderson in '29:
rag stride, barrelhouse—they said
you sounded like you'd played
with dance bands. Hell, you sounded
like a dance band by yourself.
                Rough
as Diddy Wah Diddy, on women in song,
in the jailhouse now, with Gus Gannon:
"..liked to drink and fight, got me so drunk..."
Gus hung onto you to take him home.
                  Fifty

bucks a session from Paramount,
rent parties, and too fast
at cutting sessions, everybody cut
you loose. Maybe the drinking,

the fighting and trash talk, "broke
her jaw to keep her quiet..." you
disappeared after your last two bad sides,
A, a remake, B probably not
even you. Some say robbed and killed,
the right hand no longer fast enough
to bust jaws, others say hit
by a streetcar, wandering drunk.

> *When I die, folks, without a doubt,*
> *When I die, folks, without a doubt,*
> *You won't have to do nothin' but pour me out.*

Dock Boggs
—February 7, 1898 – February 7, 1971

A big bird slams into the window. Dock Boggs
is singing:
>   *Oh the easiest thing I've ever done*
>   *was sleeping in the pines.*
The dark lab barks. For weeks, feathers
will be stuck on the window. I, who have
slept in the shortleaf pines of Missouri,
and in the boughs of Douglas fir get up
to peer out my window at the yellow-billed
cuckoo, stunned or dead on the lawn.
In the song of the cuckoo, she's a pretty
bird that warbles when she flies. Neck bent
back toward the white-spotted tail, this one
twitches and flutters when I go out to check.
Death throes or trying to escape, I can't tell,
but guess death from the quick angle of neck.

Oh the sulfur in the oil and the coal would
like to kill a man like Boggs, who thought he was out
for good in the promo shot from '29: fedora, suit,
banjo on his knee, looking sharp enough to cut
>   *forty miles through the rock*
>   *sixty through the sand*
On contract and playing holiness songs
from 27 through 31, he was soon back
in the mines, back in church, back
with Roscoe Holcomb, Wade Ward, Banjo Bill
in the vaults, no better off for twenty sides
on a defunct label and the old rub alcohol
blues in the back of his mind. Hot corn, cold
corn and bring along a jimmyjohn of gas

for peak oil on the day you die—1971
by all estimates. *Once I had a mother & father*
In a cottage by the sea, you sing, your shoes l
laced up so tight in that old photo that when
they rediscovered you forty years later
you sing a fifth lower. Wise County still got
hard luck blues, got moonshine stills ,
prizefight money, careless love, and a taste
for tupelo honey. Wise country's got diddly
in up picking style to match yours, flown away
like my cuckoo, who when I look again
has shaken off, not this mortal coil, but daze
of tempered glass to never if the song be believed,
holler cuckoo till the first day of July. But truths
in songs are only true in song. The cuckoo lays
its eggs in other's nests it's true, but also raises
cowbird young often as not. So consider, Oh Lord,
your servant, Dock, who sings:
> *The hardest thing I ever done*
> *was keepin' pork chops off my mind.*

Nocturne Moderne

Three AM clicks in to the castanets
of electrical switches fibrillating.
The furnace blows a lukewarm
narrative by Browning. My last
marriage: I stoop to dream,
but who passed without much the same
automatic smile. Refrigerator
cutting in, I realize. And on the long,
slipper-clad trek downstairs, past
the violent and tasteless neighbors,
I am called to remember in fond detail
each time the solenoids of love
failed to close properly, or seized
switching on the heat some August night.

Gastão Bueno Lobo

b. 1891, Campos, Rio d e Janeiro; d. 3 June 1939 by ingestion of
hydrochloric acid, his waltz *"Se Recordar É Viver"* (If
Remembering Is Living),….discovered in the pocket of the jacket
he was wearing. …
  —Jorge Mello, in *Musica Braziliensis* Investigations

The man who brought the banjo to Brazil,
who brought the Hawaiian slide, the Dobro,
he thinks the *labios rubios* murmur like birds
but do not speak of him.
     The *cumparsa,*
that little parade of miseries that is tango,
that is fado and the crying of *Hawainitas*—
he will unmask it.
     In his jacket, the waltz
he wrote says no. *If to remember is
to live*, shall we remember the man who brought
the orphan boy home, who taught him the cuehlo
and guitar, took him to Spain, to Django in Paris,
to Le Chantilly and the caravan the gypsy kept.

Later, after the public quarrels, after
young Oscar left with the Black Flower's band,
he went home, abandoned the four beat
swing for the choros, the waltzes and tangos he loved.
I am that I die sang the crying guitar,
in Rio, no longer swimming in a sea
of roses but asking *Que Vachacé* in the gaze
of *la criollita*. Let me translate your country
lunfardo. Whatcha gonna do,
good wolf? wolf noir? Record the tango
Cumparsita again? Arranger for the radio, fixer
of bad lines, fix yourself. Rewrite the *pagina gris,*

the grey page of your life.
                              That boy you raised
never believed sad borderland waltzes. He came home
to local fame, to teach that swing he loved,
to marriage and film roles as the sidekick,
the dancing leader of a band. It doesn't matter
whether he blamed himself for you. How could he know
your need to hurt? How? It wasn't you
he had to leave behind, but the words
to those old songs, the dying rhythms everyone
thinks so beautiful and sad. Now who's
El Presumido, the conceited one, the pimp
to sound who scours his throat of words?

Lunch at Jams Grill, Omaha, Nebraska

for Rick Barba, Richard Dooling, Richard Duggin, and
Brent Spencer, the "we" of the poem.

"We have come here Friday on a whim,"
I say. "Say, waited on by Angela."
Say she explains the specials on the run
from serving Coronas with lime, tequila.

By the time I've written these few lines
on my napkin with a borrowed pen
she's brought my special in record time
and gone to serve the lawyer at the end

of the bar. I never liked him anyway.
"This ain't no *bare and ruined choir where late
the sweet birds sang*," we hear him say.
"We're all lawyers too," I lie. "We hate

guys like you." Angela says "Eat your food,
or I'll have to tell the cook it's just no good."

Charlie Christian and the Birth of the Hip

...every one of these rills and young rivers
is fretting the air into music....
        —John Muir, "The Range of Light"

1.

I think of the dust of the Ozarks,
the mines of Joplin and Poplar Bluff,
the woods and rivers of my youth,
how we poor stood forever in our doorways:
Dallas or Centerville, East St. Louis
or Lower Hicksville—how we move out and on.

        Daddy Rocks you,
Lonnie-like, close to the theme.
Seven finds you on a homemade
ax of cigar box and wire...*Come Eleven*,
you're taking lessons same as T-Bone,
Breakfast Feud, or cutting session.
        What you need, besides
a sanatorium, is not Alphonso Trent's band—
probably Minton's ... something East.
        LA's not even
ready to happen, and in delta
shotgun shacks, the leather back
seats of cream Hudsons, or sagging
hillbilly porches, your audience—
army brats, tennis pros, frat rats—
are being conceived, born listening
to your horn-like sustain.

2.

Not far from Hughes's Joplin, Anna Mae
Winburn's rhythm section: hi-hat cuts out

chords you comp on ballads. In border towns
of wet and dry counties, flat land gives
religion and music revival. Somebody says,
"You need something, man, and you
got to, right now, get to New York
and out of this territory band."

In Texas, in Texas, the once
or twice I've been there—
sun on white rocks, a bird
singing in the hill country,
a dark, flat spill of dry
cloud north of Dallas—always bad
weather. But for you, Charlie,
in the thirties, so weirdly
studious in photos you make
Eliot look robust, what the hell
must jukes have rendered you?

No hip writers closer than the Hudson.
Hart Crane dies in '33.
The fugitives move to New York
and leave again with your fellow
consumptive, Tate. But they don't
know from Stevens saying "The Man
With the Blue Guitar" is no one at all:
not a Picasso, and surely not
you in Benny's band. So how he gets
one thing right, I can't say:

> *Things as they are.*
> *are changed upon the blue guitar.*

Wordy, but essentially correct:
        Changes, changes on the blue guitar

John Clare, Bring Your Fiddle

John Clare, bring your fiddle. We're playing
the VFW tonight. Bring the one too fine
for rowdy clubs and peasant dances.
This crowd's too old for damage, the Dusty
Miller and his wife showered and tired
of laying into one another with sack and broom.

Behind them, retired professors, veterans
of forgotten wars, bearers of renamed diseases—
no longer able to remember the words "episode,"
"shell shocked." Fiddle and guitar songs
stagger in from the Spain and Helpstone,
village maids made mortal again, no nymphs
or fauns behind buck brush in my fields.

Farm work and soldiering, tutoring the idle—
all dangerous work that puts one under care.
Music's too important for professionals.
Yellow-jacket sting on my fretting finger gave me
new double stops, a finger wide as my thumb
to bridge two strings. I'm girding on the Johns—
you and Fahey—in a tuning named for the Crimean
town that charged the Light Brigade with ruin.

War and music, the minstrel boy with his father's,
tunes we think we've learned, but find blunted
from playing the wrong key all these years.
You and the glover's boy go in and out of fashion,
but the songs remain, and the woman wears
her apron low or high depending on the season.

Summer ends with prejudice. Grasshoppers
and grapes turn color on the vines, the clusters

so wet wasps can't fly. This one can sting.
Let's trade eights on Shady Grove,
march off to the bosom of our fathers,
village minstrels whoever they may be.
Lean closer, I'll retune my guitar
to your fiddle.

All Saints: South Omaha

The odor beneath smoke,
that bright honey
in a stone so long buried,
still erases traffic
within school children,
their suits composed
of yellow rain slickers
and hats canted into
their napes.
Parish children
wear their Polish and Irish
neighborhoods
across underground waterways.
Small birds fool them
from the storm drains.
Squirrels and raccoons
watch them flavor rye grass
and fescue plugged into the plumb
slope above their playground.
The sweet ghost balanced
on the swings, herself
a dirge among them

Festival

Late at night the coroner's assistant
speaks to the drowned, she tells me.
When the fleet comes in for the annual
parade and festival each spring,
she must work, due to some chemistry
the dead know, gas formed in the tissues
set free by the pounding resonance
of heavy screws, bearing, as the locals say
the sailors upriver to spawn.

Tom Sawyer's aunt sent
a launch out to fire over the water,
to release loaves of bread
buttered with silver he spent.
If I am a *pore drownt angel,*
it is this free beer that made me
overshoot Cairo in the night.
I tap the side of the abused bottle
in what must be a model for corpses

sunk in river silt. Bubbles rise.
Maybe this is why on her first night
out in years, this girl tells me
her secret, why the bridge keeper
knew to share his knowledge:
how floaters hang up in the buttress
and the sheriff screamed at him
for God's sake not to look —
the head swelled up like a bull's,

like a ratfish reeled up too suddenly
sighing through its gills. It's late
and she is still talking.

I can't rise clear of the weight
of her voice, this lounge and my friend's
bad band. The clarinet and guitar
silt up with blue light and the clean
dead smell of disinfectant.

Bucky Takes Time Off

The air is pine, the lake weak tea, the stream
as thick with poison oak as fencerows we
kids could never stay out of. Shift the wind
another twelve degrees and this could be
east slope, the Siskiyous in September,
lower Coast Range or the Blues—a range
named with local wind conditions in mind.

A jaded horse's hips crack and it farts
itself across the switchbacks to the tune
of drum machines mercifully trapped inside
one teen-aged rider's half-shaved head
by earphones. His stepfather sits familiarly
and looks embarrassed for the horses' pain—
his own, he knows, tomorrow in the thighs
and groin. He's out of shape and practice now
for most things. You can see him concentrate
on the lisping call of Clark's nutcrackers—
a local jay, camp robber, means of distribution
for the lodgepole pine. Fuck them both
I think, as they and seven others ride
around a bend and out of sight. My own
stepson is driving his mother to tears while I
take three guilty hours to fish this brook.

Water cress is strong this late, but I bite.
My form is passable, the delivery of the fly
has all the finesse of UPS. Forgiving
trout first mouth then bite and I have a mint-
lined canvas creel, but release the two I land.
Is mint and memory catch enough? Three
hours, four bites, no errors in the poison
oak I warn a mother and two boys off.

Two weeks later, cleaning the garage, I crush
the creel of dried mint under my hand and scent
sun's declination. My wife worries I ride
her son too hard. I still blame him for pain
that's none of my business. He avoids me.
I avoid my wife. Here are dried leaves,
needle of lodgepole that won't grow within a days
drive of where I now live. Here's the leader,
here the hook set in my finger, just
past the barb. I push it through
and rummage tool chests for wire cutters
someone is always using. Dammit-to-Hell!
I whisper, twice. Don't ask me why I'm so happy

At the Heartland Cafe

Carol says "His automatic's really cool,"
blows her coffee "but that .38
is one sweet weapon." She got state
twice, went to nationals. "Only a fool
like Bucky forgets to tighten his scope down—
sighting it in and it damn near tore
his nose off. God, what a mess. He wore
that gauze like Nicholson in China Town."

But Sandy's not so sure. "You know my Jeff
wakes up hard. I wouldn't want to excite
him when he's sleeping. If I just snap my fingers,
he jumps up and throws the covers off.
When I ask what if the kids run in some night,
he says 'I won't shoot no two-foot intruders.'"

i'm not he is

i tell the lady i'm not leland he is
so she won't call me that. she laughs again.
i put the groceries in my little wagon
is red for him to ride in. he says to tease
me like a brother that old store lady
won't believe you if you hear me don't
you know what your name is think its leland
shows you don't i am till we're both crazy

in the nuthouse. but not the way the doctor
says does he tell you do things? no
but yes he's the bad one i'm the good
leland even gets him drink of water.
doctor says don't say nothing, so
i won't, just try to get home with this food.

Pawnshops

The best ones don't stint on yellow
paint and neon. As if you need reminding
their business is BUY * SELL * TRADE.

Guitars hang from wires and rafters
ripening like dry salamis in dust
from scattered boxes of tools,

televisions and stereos, in the very
air which says by touch and smell
there are no crimes here but murder

and timidity. Go in, but not
for the silver, pieces heavy
as the knives from scimitar

to surgical, bought on speculation.
Stare past the obsolete cameras, flawless
cowboy boots you could wear home

before you found the blood inside.
Touch the thing that takes your eye
though the owner clears his throat to say

you break it, you buy it.
But it's afternoon, Wednesday, and you
have money and free time. Ignore him

If you don't know better than him
what that Les Paul you're holding's worth,
you've got no business here, deserve

no deal, to leave ashamed and broke.

Tell him to plug the damn thing in, and when
he sends the skeptical boy out of the cage

let them know if they don't want to hear it loud
they shouldn't sell electrics. Bet him
he doesn't know who Mary Ford is.

Offer half their asking. Anything
you buy here is a spare. Remember that.
You've got as good TV at home, but the wife—

always the wife, the kids—wants one
in the bedroom. As if it were their
business. It's not. It's a matter of respect.

It's been good talking. You may be back.

Three Day California Honky Tonk Weekend

Hey mister bartender, please don't you be so slow.
I got time for one more round and a six-pack to go.
                        — Hank Thompson

Sixty five cent shots of Louis' bar booze
nursed a working class binge through one night.
Harder than it seems, keeping propped up
with only a week's paycheck between you
and the drive home to unpaid rent, a wife
perfectly wise to the three whores,
the half-furnished farmhouse outside Cotati.

The last day a light wholly pure
bounces up off flattened grass, regimental
miles of vineyard, through a window
unaccountably clean and onto the ceiling.
The heavy one stands over you, full of schnapps
and indignation over the man who stiffed her.
You can't say in whose name you pay her —

certainly not his, a face you couldn't
tell from your own, swollen blue in the mirror.
You tell her a good time drives business sense
right out of some men's heads. Now the hard
considerations: when to go home, why Spanish
has no different word for sky than heaven,
where you heard the song about *corazon* and *alma*.

Also interrupted, that double flip of the stomach
that would be panic if this were not still
the valley, if it were, say Reno again, the whole
paycheck gone — would be fear if the body

could bear it and if it were not so familiar.
But this is home, or just as well. Outside that clear
window the Mexican pickers call, working

this vineyard slowly as geologic force building
toward earthquake, as weather waiting for flood.
The earth pulls this way and that under uncertain sky.
The dark skin and clothes of the immigrants
spread over the land. The language you misunderstand
sings of such forces above and below
as will tear this state off the map.

The Fly Wallet

Full grain flaps snap crisply
shut on felt pages dangling
nymphs and coachmen like pressed
flowers waiting for a touch
of glycerin. The flies I use,
not hand-tied, set up with a quick
spray of silicone and keep
better in their plastic box.
This thrift store wallet
insists on split cane—foolish,
like an old man's fondness
for the ridiculous car of his youth.

All of his nymphs will unravel
like wicker chairs in the sun,
the hook turn brittle and barb
drop off when hits come hard.
He's left only finesse, a gallant
apology when he reaches in his pocket
to find, instead of credit cards,
this anachronism, its delicate
ledger of imitations spilling
onto the glass case.

He came to this boutique to buy
his young lover a dress
like the one his dead wife wore.
It's coming into style again.
The girl behind the counter doesn't
fish, though she smiles
through that fog of scent
he would never brave when married.
He keeps explaining this.

He is terribly sorry.

Having once found bottom in a river
he knew, he thought all time
borrowed from the deep pockets of trousers
he never bothered getting wet,
thought he could wade shallows home.

I found this log of his expeditions
under clothing-by-the-pound, no one
to teach me blue flies, these white
moths hovering at the edge of mildew,
what this black and straw weave
salmon fly meant to say
with its whistling flight.

Survivors

Hungry even when food's no good,
the godawful son they saved from scarlet
fever claws the bank for red clay
smooth enough to eat while Riley and Edna
search the streambed for what they call
arry heads, chipped from white-veined chert.

Weeks later I will scribe with the heel
of my hand a crescent in the even
coat of river silt blanking the windshield
of their '78 Pontiac. Black moon
in a powderwhite sky, outhouse cutout,
it will illuminate, will show me:

Blankets twisted out of sleeping bag over-
lying camp stove and lantern; tent
pegs still attached to parachute cord
stitching pots to ripstop to headrest
to sponge rubber poking erectile through vinyl
seatcovers — all coated with gray

silt the color of that conceptual art piece
I saw six weeks ago at the traveling
exhibit underwritten by and featuring
the work of a famous actor whose piece was
actually good. All that night as I lay beneath
the open window and a breeze tepid

as my own tongue laved my face, I kept
waking to the storm that would not build.
Not the moon, not plates of the earth,
the huge domes of air sliding across each
other like mating whales — this wall of water

pushing through clay banks is what

I dreamed. Enough to clear the light
pressure knocking at my temples, to wash
chips of chert and granite down into the next
blue pool cut in limestone. Folks awakened
like me by what they never asked for
stand around and talk it over. Or pile

the gear they've gathered up around the house
and borrowed from Edna's sister whose roses
the boy ruined and blamed it on the dog —
pile it into the car they owe on and that costs
them thirty cents a mile they can't afford to drive
just in time to save it all from being swept off,

but can't start that Bonneville anyway, the roar
so loud Riley can't hear her shouting at him to go
so he does just to get her out of there, and they
run up the access road in plenty of time to watch
it rise across the wheel wells
and for him to say "I didn't flood it. Must of

got the distributor wet." And the boy, already
looking in runoff ditchwater blood-thick
with red silt for drowned frogs, has somehow
held onto the flashlight, making neither of them
think about saving the charge, but both remember
the arrow heads which even now the current
rakes against the windshield.

Art Homer has taught at the University of Nebraska at Omaha Writer's Workshop since 1982. He is the recipient of a 1998 NEA Writing Fellowship, a 1995 Individual Artist Fellowship from Nebraska Arts Council, and a Regents Professorship from the University of Nebraska. Homer's nonfiction book *The Drownt Boy: An Ozark Tale* (University of Missouri Press, 1994) was published as a finalist for the AWP Award in Creative Nonfiction. His previous poetry collections include *Sight is No Carpenter* (2005) and *Skies of Such Valuable Glass* (1990).

CPSIA information can be obtained at www.ICGtesting.com
Printed in the USA
LVOW051459090612

285389LV00001B/16/P